Beesville Books

beesvillebooks.com

ISBN: 9781707613090

what better way

to start or end your day
than with an
inspirational
QUOTE

1. Add today's date on the "Date" line
2. Enjoy your quote
3. Read your related question below the "Date" line
4. Write your answer / deepest thoughts!

1.

BE AT WAR WITH YOUR
VICES, AT PEACE WITH
YOUR NEIGHBORS,
AND LET EVERY NEW
YEAR FIND YOU A
BETTER MAN.

BENJAMIN FRANKLIN

Date _____

What is your BIG New Year's Resolution?

2.

WITH THE FEARFUL
STRAIN THAT IS ON ME
NIGHT AND DAY,
IF I DID NOT LAUGH
I SHOULD DIE.

ABRAHAM LINCOLN

Date _____

What strains on your life are you facing right now?

What major decision did you make today?

3.

NOTHING IS MORE
DIFFICULT, AND
THEREFORE MORE
PRECIOUS, THAN THE
ABILITY TO DECIDE.

NAPOLEON BONAPARTE

What area in your life do you think you may
need to speed up, or slow down?

4.

IT DOES NOT MATTER
HOW SLOWLY YOU GO
AS LONG AS YOU DO
NOT STOP.

CONFUCIUS

5.

DO GOOD TO YOUR FRIENDS TO KEEP THEM, TO YOUR ENEMIES TO WIN THEM.

BENJAMIN FRANKLIN

What kind thing could you do or say to someone you've fallen out with?

6.

NEVER INJURE A FRIEND, EVEN IN JEST.

CICERO

When was the last time you said something hurtful to a friend and wished you could take it back?

Date _____

Are you grateful to be free?

_____

_____

_____

_____

_____

_____

7.

HE WHO IS
BRAVE IS FREE.

SENECA

Date _____

Are you letting fear hold you back?

_____

_____

_____

_____

_____

_____

8.

EVERYTHING YOU'VE
EVER WANTED
IS ON THE
OTHER SIDE
OF FEAR.

GEORGE ADDAIR

9.

THERE IS NO MORE
MISERABLE HUMAN
BEING THAN ONE IN
WHOM NOTHING
IS HABITUAL BUT
INDECISION.

WILLIAM JAMES

Are you good or bad at making up your mind
and sticking with a decision?

10.

HE WHO
TALKS MORE
IS SOONER
EXHAUSTED.

LAO TZU

Are you, in general, more of a talker
or a listener?

When you fail at something, how long does it take for you get going again?

11.

OUR GREATEST GLORY
IS NOT IN NEVER
FALLING, BUT IN
RISING EVERY
TIME WE FALL.

CONFUCIUS

Do you take time out, every day, to play?

12.

GAMES LUBRICATE
THE BODY
AND THE MIND.

BENJAMIN FRANKLIN

13.

DO YOU WANT TO KNOW WHO YOU ARE? DON'T ASK. ACT! ACTION WILL DELINEATE AND DEFINE YOU.

THOMAS JEFFERSON

Do your actions speak louder than your words?

14.

THE BEGINNING IS THE MOST IMPORTANT PART OF THE WORK.

PLATO

Do you agree with this? If so, why?

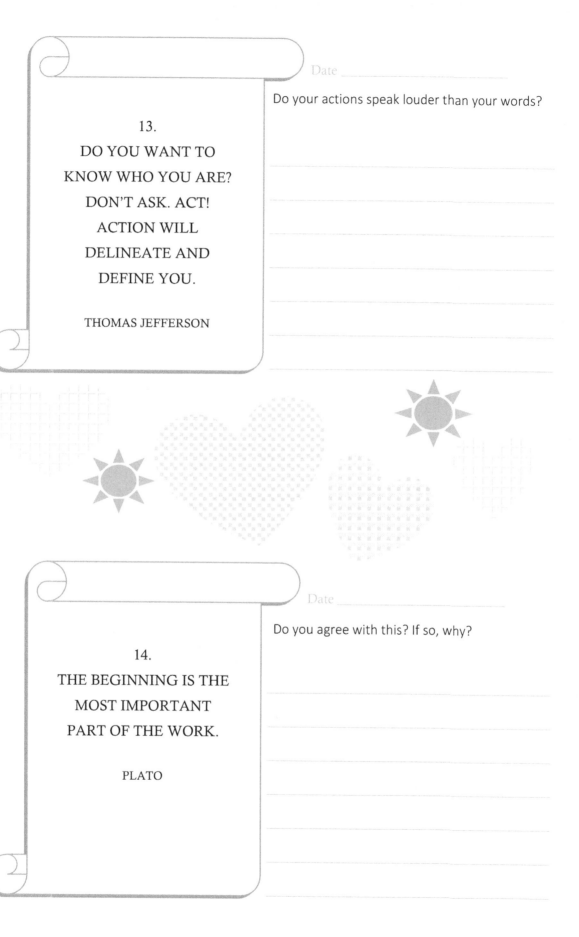

Are you a hoarder, or a giver?

15.

HE WHO CANNOT GIVE ANYTHING AWAY CANNOT FEEL ANYTHING EITHER.

FRIEDRICH NIETZSCHE

What seeds to you plant that foster your personal growth?

16.

DON'T JUDGE EACH DAY BY THE HARVEST YOU REAP BUT BY THE SEEDS THAT YOU PLANT.

ROBERT LOUIS STEVENSON

17.

WE CAN COMPLAIN
BECAUSE ROSE BUSHES
HAVE THORNS, OR
REJOICE BECAUSE
THORN BUSHES HAVE
ROSES.

ABRAHAM LINCOLN

Which side of the rose bush theory are you on?

Date

18.

GO ON AND
IMPROVE IN
EVERYTHING
WORTHY.

JOHN ADAMS

What is the most worthwhile thing have you improved upon recently?

19.

MOST MEN SEEM TO LIVE ACCORDING TO SENSE RATHER THAN REASON.

ST. THOMAS AQUINAS

Date _____

What was the last nonsensical thing you did?

_____
_____
_____
_____
_____
_____
_____

20.

THE HARDER THE CONFLICT, THE MORE GLORIOUS THE TRIUMPH.

THOMAS PAINE

Date _____

What conflict and triumph did you overcome today?

_____
_____
_____
_____
_____
_____
_____

21.

SOMETIMES THE
PEOPLE WITH THE
WORST PAST,
CREATE THE BEST
FUTURE.

UMAR IBN AL-KHATTAB

Date _____

Have you recently overcome something from your past? If so, what was it?

22.

WHEREVER THERE
IS A HUMAN BEING,
THERE IS AN
OPPORTUNITY
FOR A KINDNESS.

SENECA

Date _____

What act of kindness did you show today? And to whom?

23.

NO DUTY THE
EXECUTIVE HAD TO
PERFORM WAS SO
TRYING AS TO PUT THE
RIGHT MAN IN THE
RIGHT PLACE.

THOMAS JEFFERSON

At work, are you the boss? If so, what's your best quality that you're proud of?

24.

MAGIC IS BELIEVING
IN YOURSELF,
IF YOU CAN DO THAT,
YOU CAN MAKE
ANYTHING HAPPEN.

JOHANN WOLFGANG
VON GOETHE

Do you believe in your abilities?

Do you consider yourself a virtuous person?

25.

VIRTUE IS RELATIVE
TO THE ACTIONS
AND AGES OF EACH
OF US IN ALL
THAT WE DO.

PLATO

What's your favorite kind of book?

26.

AN INVESTMENT IN
KNOWLEDGE PAYS
THE BEST INTEREST.

BENJAMIN FRANKLIN

Date _____

How much of a perfectionist are you?

27.

BETTER A LITTLE
THAT IS WELL DONE,
THAN A GREAT DEAL
IMPERFECTLY.

PLATO

Date _____

How well do you manage your budget?

28.

IT IS THRIFTY TO
PREPARE TODAY
FOR THE WANTS
OF TOMORROW.

AESOP

29.
PESSIMISM LEADS TO WEAKNESS, OPTIMISM TO POWER.

WILLIAM JAMES

In general, are you an optimist or a pessimist?

30.
YOU YOURSELF, AS MUCH AS ANYBODY IN THE ENTIRE UNIVERSE DESERVE YOUR LOVE AND AFFECTION.

GAUTAMA BUDDHA

Do you think you're worthy of love and affection?

31.

LIFE IS TEN PERCENT WHAT HAPPENS TO YOU AND NINETY PERCENT HOW YOU RESPOND TO IT.

LOU HOLTZ

How do you respond to things that happen to you on a daily basis?

32.

HAPPINESS IS THE ONLY GOOD. THE TIME TO BE HAPPY IS NOW. THE PLACE TO BE HAPPY IS HERE. THE WAY TO BE HAPPY IS TO MAKE OTHERS SO.

ROBERT INGERSOLL

Do you spend more time making yourself happy, or others happy ... or equally so?

Date _____

Do you agree with Ben?

33.

TELL ME AND
I FORGET.
TEACH ME AND
I REMEMBER.
INVOLVE ME
AND I LEARN.

BENJAMIN FRANKLIN

Date _____

Do you think ignorance is bliss?

34.

REAL KNOWLEDGE
IS TO KNOW THE
EXTENT OF ONE'S
IGNORANCE.

CONFUCIUS

35.

CHARACTER DEVELOPS
ITSELF IN THE STREAM
OF LIFE.

JOHANN WOLFGANG
VON GOETHE

Date _____

What are your best character traits?

36.

PEOPLE WHO ARE UNABLE
TO MOTIVATE
THEMSELVES MUST BE
CONTENT WITH
MEDIOCRITY, NO MATTER
HOW IMPRESSIVE THEIR
OTHER TALENTS.

ANDREW CARNEGIE

Date _____

Are you self-motivated when inspiration hits?

37.

NO UNTROUBLED DAY HAS EVER DAWNED FOR ME.

SENECA

Date _____

Do you have the same sentiment as Seneca?

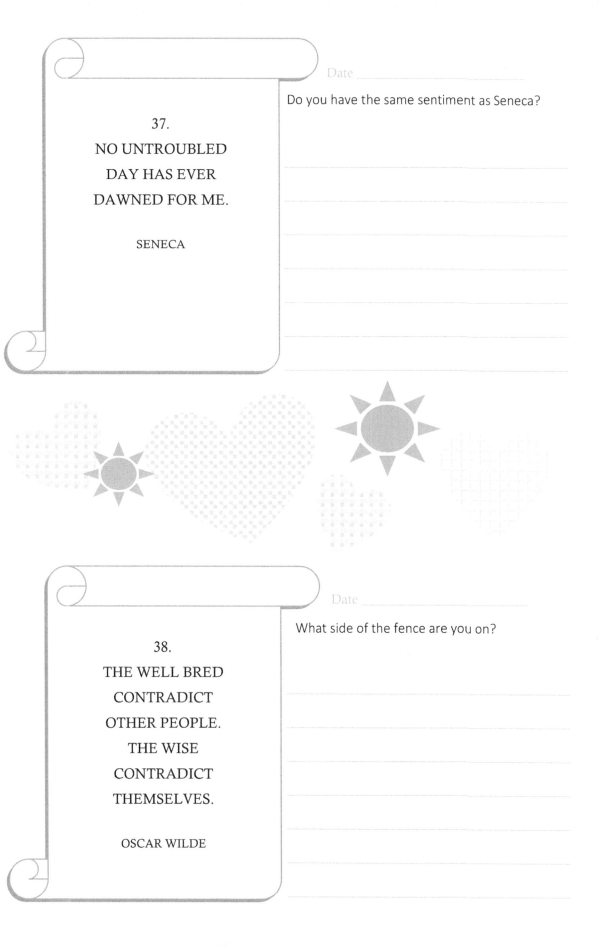

38.

THE WELL BRED CONTRADICT OTHER PEOPLE. THE WISE CONTRADICT THEMSELVES.

OSCAR WILDE

Date _____

What side of the fence are you on?

39.

MOST PEOPLE NEVER
RUN FAR ENOUGH ON
THEIR FIRST WIND TO
REALIZE THEY'VE GOT
A SECOND.

WILLIAM JAMES

Do you ever experience a "second wind" when tackling projects?

40.

IF IT DOESN'T
CHALLENGE YOU,
IT WON'T CHANGE
YOU.

UNKNOWN

What was a challenge you faced today and did it change you?

Do you have a soulmate?

41.

FRIENDSHIP IS A
SINGLE SOUL
DWELLING IN TWO
BODIES.

ARISTOTLE

Do you agree with Abe?

42.

IF YOU WISH TO WIN A
MAN OVER TO YOUR
IDEAS, FIRST MAKE
HIM YOUR FRIEND.

ABRAHAM LINCOLN

Date _____

Did you miss out on taking a chance today?

43.

BEWARE OF
MISSING CHANCES,
OTHERWISE IT MAY BE
ALTOGETHER
TOO LATE
SOME DAY.

FRANZ LISZT

Date _____

Do you trust people too much, or too little?

44.

ALL MEN PROFESS
HONESTY AS LONG AS
THEY CAN. TO BELIEVE
ALL MEN HONEST
WOULD BE FOLLY. TO
BELIEVE NONE SO IS
SOMETHING WORSE.

JOHN QUINCY ADAMS

45.

**WONDER IS THE
DESIRE FOR
KNOWLEDGE.**

ST. THOMAS AQUINAS

What wonderous thing did you discover today?

46.

**IT IS A ROUGH ROAD
THAT LEADS
TO THE HEIGHTS
OF GREATNESS.**

SENECA

Have you been—or are you on—a tough road right now?

47.
IN MATTERS OF STYLE,
SWIM WITH
THE CURRENT;
IN MATTERS OF
PRINCIPLE, STAND
LIKE A ROCK.

THOMAS JEFFERSON

Date _____

Do you stand by your principles?

48.
CORRECTION DOES
MUCH, BUT
ENCOURAGEMENT
DOES MORE.

JOHANN WOLFGANG
VON GOETHE

Date _____

Do you agree with Johann?

What does Plato mean?

49.

TWICE AND THRICE
OVER, AS THEY SAY,
GOOD IS IT TO REPEAT
AND REVIEW
WHAT IS GOOD.

PLATO

What skills do you have that are in demand?

50.

ABILITY WILL NEVER
CATCH UP WITH THE
DEMAND FOR IT.

CONFUCIUS

How much stuff do you "put off" until later?

51.
YOU MAY DELAY,
BUT TIME WILL NOT.

BENJAMIN FRANKLIN

Do you know what Thomas' middle name is?
(answer upside down, below)

52.
THE VALUE OF AN IDEA
LIES IN THE USING OF
IT.

THOMAS A. EDISON

Alva

53.

RESULTS HAPPEN
OVER TIME,
NOT OVERNIGHT.
WORK HARD,
STAY CONSISTENT,
AND BE PATIENT.

UNKNOWN

Date _____

How patient are you when working toward finishing a project?

54.

IT'S NOT BECAUSE
THINGS ARE DIFFICULT
THAT WE DARE NOT
VENTURE. IT'S
BECAUSE WE DARE
NOT VENTURE THAT
THEY ARE DIFFICULT.

SENECA

Date _____

How adventurous are you?

Did you have a "light bulb" moment today?

55.

THE NOBLEST
PLEASURE IS THE JOY
OF UNDERSTANDING.

LEONARDO DA VINCI

Do you sometimes think you're the only sane person on the planet? ;-)

56.

I CAN CALCULATE THE
MOTION OF HEAVENLY
BODIES, BUT NOT THE
MADNESS OF PEOPLE.

ISAAC NEWTON

How well do you prepare in advance?

57.

GIVE ME SIX HOURS TO
CHOP DOWN A TREE
AND I WILL SPEND
THE FIRST FOUR
SHARPENING THE AXE.

ABRAHAM LINCOLN

Do you find yourself compromising a lot?

58.

COMPROMISE MAKES
A GOOD UMBRELLA
BUT A POOR ROOF.

JAMES RUSSELL LOWELL

What fear did you quash today?

59.

HE WHO HAS
CONQUERED DOUBT
AND FEAR
HAS CONQUERED
FAILURE.

JAMES LANE ALLEN

What did experience teach you today?

60.

EXPERIENCE IS THE
TEACHER OF ALL
THINGS.

JULIUS CAESAR

61.

THE GREATEST TEST OF COURAGE ON EARTH IS TO BEAR DEFEAT WITHOUT LOSING HEART.

ROBERT INGERSOLL

Do you lose heart easily when things don't go as well as planned?

62.

LIFE IS THE CONTINUOUS ADJUSTMENT OF INTERNAL RELATIONS TO EXTERNAL RELATIONS.

HERBERT SPENCER

How well do you adjust to daily changes?

Do you marvel at just how many shades of green there are in your trees?

63.

IN ALL THINGS OF
NATURE, THERE IS
SOMETHING OF THE
MARVELOUS.

ARISTOTLE

Do you let perfectionism get in the way of getting the job done?

64.

PERFECTION?
BEING THE
MOST HUMAN
YOU CAN BE.

GIOVANNI MORASSUTTI

65.

LEARNING IS NOT
ATTAINED BY CHANCE,
IT MUST BE SOUGHT
FOR WITH ARDOR AND
ATTENDED TO WITH
DILIGENCE.

ABIGAIL ADAMS

When you're learning something new, do you finish the whole course / book?

66.

TACT IS THE ABILITY
TO DESCRIBE OTHERS
AS THEY SEE
THEMSELVES.

ABRAHAM LINCOLN

Do you consider yourself to be a tactful person?

67.

WE SHOULD GIVE AS WE WOULD RECEIVE, CHEERFULLY, QUICKLY, AND WITHOUT HESITATION; FOR THERE IS NO GRACE IN A BENEFIT THAT STICKS TO THE FINGERS.

SENECA

Date _____

Do you have trouble giving things away?

68.

DO NOT BITE AT THE BAIT OF PLEASURE, TILL YOU KNOW THERE IS NO HOOK BENEATH IT.

THOMAS JEFFERSON

Date _____

Are you impulsive?

Are you careful at what you laugh at in the presence of others?

69.

NOTHING SHOWS A MAN'S CHARACTER MORE THAN WHAT HE LAUGHS AT.

JOHANN WOLFGANG
VON GOETHE

Do you agree with Johann? It's like "beauty is in the eye of the beholder," right?

70.

EVERYTHING HAS BEAUTY, BUT NOT EVERYONE SEES IT.

JOHANN WOLFGANG
VON GOETHE

How well do you know yourself?

71.

THERE ARE THREE
THINGS EXTREMELY
HARD: STEEL,
A DIAMOND,
AND TO
KNOW ONE'S SELF.

BENJAMIN FRANKLIN

Do you do your best every chance you get?

72.

YOU DON'T WANT TO
LOOK BACK AND
KNOW YOU COULD
HAVE DONE BETTER.

UNKNOWN

73.

THE CREATION OF
A THOUSAND FORESTS
IS IN ONE ACORN.

RALPH WALDO EMERSON

Date _____

What analogy can you come up with?

74.

THROW OFF YOUR
WORRIES WHEN YOU
THROW OFF YOUR
CLOTHES AT NIGHT.

NAPOLEON BONAPARTE

Date _____

Do you "let everything go" at the day's end?

Are you creating your own future?

75.

THE BEST WAY TO
PREDICT THE FUTURE
IS TO CREATE IT.

ABRAHAM LINCOLN

Are you at peace, or conflicted?

76.

PEACE COMES
FROM WITHIN.
DO NOT SEEK IT
WITHOUT.

GAUTAMA BUDDHA

77.

NEVER TROUBLE
ANOTHER
FOR WHAT YOU CAN
DO YOURSELF.

THOMAS JEFFERSON

Do you often involve others unnecessarily in order to be helped?

78.

THE LESS ONE
HAS TO DO,
THE LESS TIME ONE
FINDS TO DO IT IN.

LORD CHESTERFIELD

Do you agree with Chesterfield?

79.

THE OBJECT
OF THE
SUPERIOR MAN IS
TRUTH.

CONFUCIUS

Date _____

Do you consider yourself to be a truthful person?

80.

PATIENCE IS BITTER,
BUT ITS FRUIT
IS SWEET.

ARISTOTLE

Date _____

Do you agree with Aristotle?

Date _____

Is your life in balance?

81.

LIFE IS A
BALANCE OF
HOLDING ON
AND
LETTING GO.

RUMI

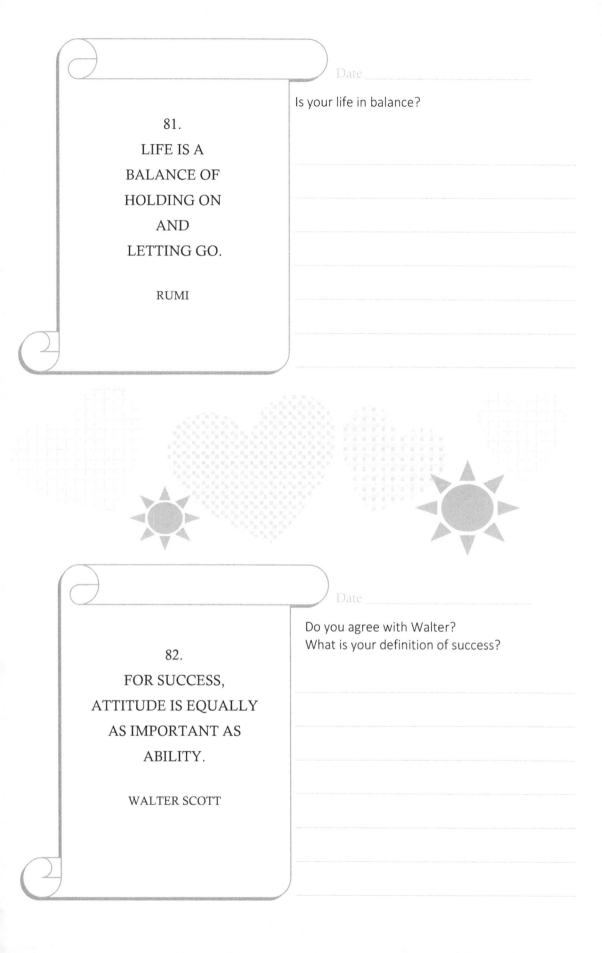

Date _____

Do you agree with Walter?
What is your definition of success?

82.

FOR SUCCESS,
ATTITUDE IS EQUALLY
AS IMPORTANT AS
ABILITY.

WALTER SCOTT

Date _____

Are you a leader, or a follower?

83.

IF YOUR ACTIONS
INSPIRE OTHERS TO
DREAM MORE, LEARN
MORE, DO MORE AND
BECOME MORE, YOU
ARE A LEADER.

JOHN QUINCY ADAMS

Date _____

Are you wise, or a fool in this respect?

84.

WISE MEN SPEAK
BECAUSE THEY HAVE
SOMETHING TO SAY;
FOOLS BECAUSE
THEY HAVE TO SAY
SOMETHING.

PLATO

85.

THE THINGS THAT
WE LOVE
TELL US
WHAT WE ARE.

ST. THOMAS AQUINAS

Date _____

Do you surround yourself with things you love?

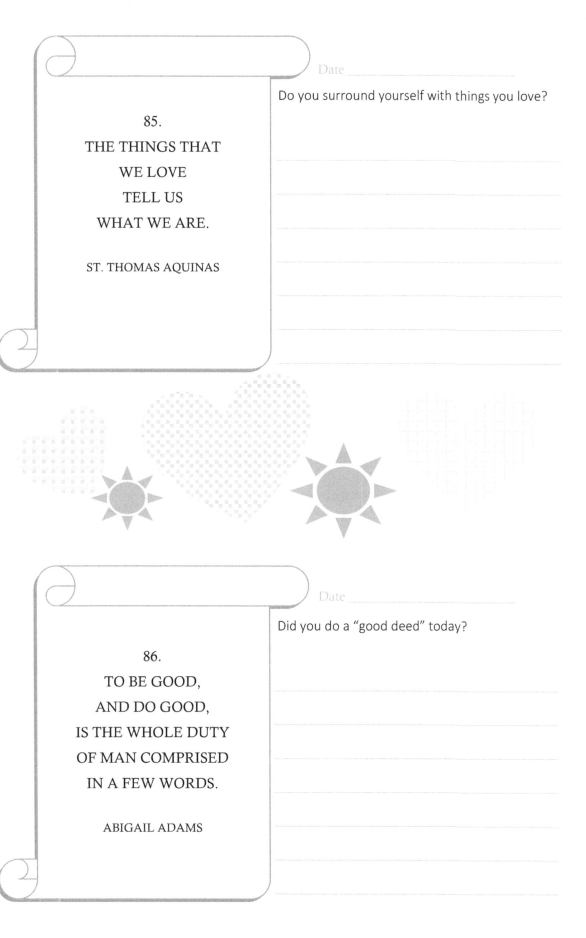

86.

TO BE GOOD,
AND DO GOOD,
IS THE WHOLE DUTY
OF MAN COMPRISED
IN A FEW WORDS.

ABIGAIL ADAMS

Date _____

Did you do a "good deed" today?

87.

BE SURE TO PUT
YOUR FEET IN THE
RIGHT PLACE,
THEN STAND FIRM.

ABRAHAM LINCOLN

Date _____

Do you stand firm after you've made a decision?

88.

ONE MAY SOMETIMES
TELL A LIE, BUT THE
GRIMACE THAT
ACCOMPANIES IT
TELLS THE TRUTH.

FRIEDRICH NIETZSCHE

Date _____

Do you disagree with Friedrich?

89.

A GEM CANNOT
BE POLISHED
WITHOUT FRICTION,
NOR A MAN
PERFECTED
WITHOUT TRIALS.

SENECA

Do you think "practice makes perfect"?

90.

ADVERTISEMENTS
CONTAIN THE ONLY
TRUTHS TO BE RELIED
ON IN A NEWSPAPER.

THOMAS JEFFERSON

Do you think this sentiment holds true today?

91.
HAPPINESS DEPENDS UPON OURSELVES.

ARISTOTLE

Date _____

Do you ever leave your happiness in someone else's hands?

92.
BEHAVIOR IS THE MIRROR IN WHICH EVERYONE SHOWS THEIR IMAGE.

JOHANN WOLFGANG VON GOETHE

Date _____

Is this a case of "do as I say, not as I do?"

93.

IF YOU WOULD
BE LOVED,
LOVE,
AND BE LOVEABLE.

BENJAMIN FRANKLIN

Date _____

Do you love yourself enough to be loved by
others?

_____

_____

_____

_____

_____

_____

94.

BE YOURSELF:
EVERYONE ELSE IS
ALREADY TAKEN.

OSCAR WILDE

Date _____

Are you true to your nature?

_____

_____

_____

_____

_____

_____

_____

95.

HE WHO OPENS
A SCHOOL DOOR
CLOSES A PRISON.

VICTOR HUGO

Do you think the 'uneducated' are more likely to land in prison?

96.

LOVE INSPIRES,
ILLUMINATES,
DESIGNATES AND
LEADS THE WAY.

MARY BAKER EDDY

Do you agree with Mary?

97.

LIFE IS SOMETHING
THAT EVERYONE
SHOULD TRY
AT LEAST ONCE.

HENRY J. TILLMAN

Date _____

Are you living your life to the fullest, or do you
hold yourself back?

98.

THERE IS NO REMEDY
FOR LOVE BUT TO LOVE
MORE.

HENRY DAVID THOREAU

Date _____

Do you think this sentiment is true?

99.

**THREE THINGS
CANNOT BE LONG
HIDDEN:
THE SUN, THE MOON
AND THE TRUTH.**

GAUTAMA BUDDHA

Date _____

Do you agree with Buddha?

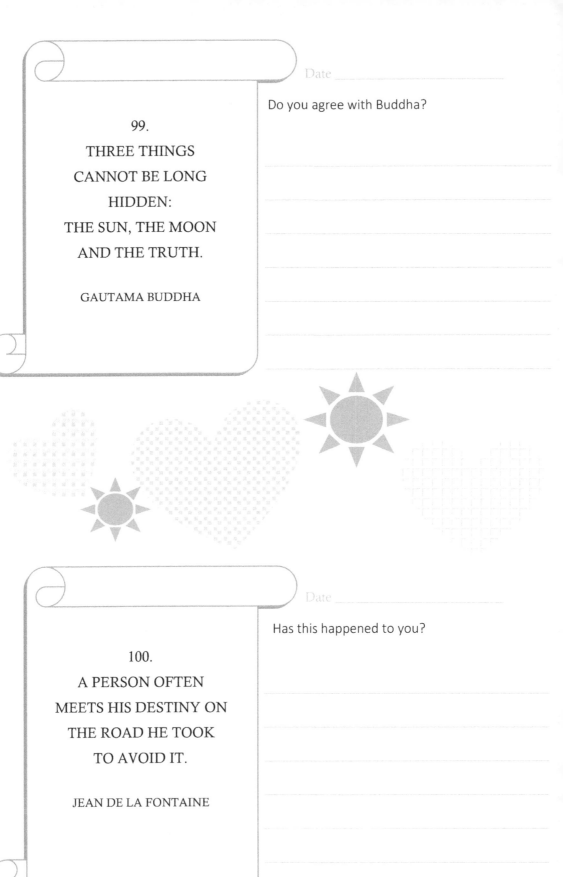

100.

**A PERSON OFTEN
MEETS HIS DESTINY ON
THE ROAD HE TOOK
TO AVOID IT.**

JEAN DE LA FONTAINE

Date _____

Has this happened to you?

Date _____

Do you consider yourself to be a negative or positive person?

101.

POSITIVE ANYTHING
IS BETTER THAN
NEGATIVE NOTHING.

ELBERT HUBBARD

Date _____

Are you a procrastinator at heart?

102.

THE SECRET OF
GETTING AHEAD IS
GETTING STARTED.

MARK TWAIN

Are you as wise as Carnegie?

103.

AS I GROW OLDER,
I PAY LESS ATTENTION
TO WHAT MEN SAY.
I JUST WATCH
WHAT THEY DO.

ANDREW CARNEGIE

Do you agree with Ibsen?

104.

THERE IS ALWAYS A
RISK IN BEING ALIVE,
AND IF YOU ARE
MORE ALIVE,
THERE IS MORE RISK.

HENRIK IBSEN

105.

TRUE HAPPINESS
IS TO ENJOY THE
PRESENT,
WITHOUT ANXIOUS
DEPENDENCE
ON THE FUTURE.

SENECA

Date _____

Are you anxious about your future?

106.

YOU HAVE YOUR WAY.
I HAVE MY WAY.
AS FOR THE RIGHT WAY,
THE CORRECT WAY,
AND THE ONLY WAY,
IT DOES NOT EXIST.

FRIEDRICH NIETZSCHE

Date _____

Do you have to have things "your way" all the time?

107.

THE TRUE SOURCE OF
OUR SUFFERING HAS
BEEN OUR TIMIDITY.
WE HAVE BEEN AFRAID
TO THINK... LET US
DARE TO READ, THINK,
SPEAK AND WRITE.

JOHN ADAMS

Are you a timid mouse, or more like a lion?

108.

TO ONE WHO HAS FAITH,
NO EXPLANATION IS
NECESSARY. TO ONE
WITHOUT FAITH,
NO EXPLANATION
IS POSSIBLE.

ST. THOMAS AQUINAS

Do you have the tendency to believe everything
you're told, or what you read?

Date _____

109.

HONESTY IS THE FIRST CHAPTER IN THE BOOK OF WISDOM.

THOMAS JEFFERSON

Do you agree with Jefferson?

Date _____

110.

I DESTROY MY ENEMIES WHEN I MAKE THEM MY FRIENDS.

ABRAHAM LINCOLN

Do you forgive easily?

111.
IT IS DURING OUR DARKEST MOMENTS THAT WE MUST FOCUS TO SEE THE LIGHT.

ARISTOTLE

When you're down, what's your favorite thing to do to pick yourself up?

112.
WHAT IS NOT STARTED TODAY IS NEVER FINISHED TOMORROW.

JOHANN WOLFGANG VON GOETHE

Don't you think this is such a clever quote?

113.

FOR A MAN TO
CONQUER HIMSELF
IS THE FIRST AND
NOBLEST OF ALL
VICTORIES.

PLATO

Date _____

What things hold you back?

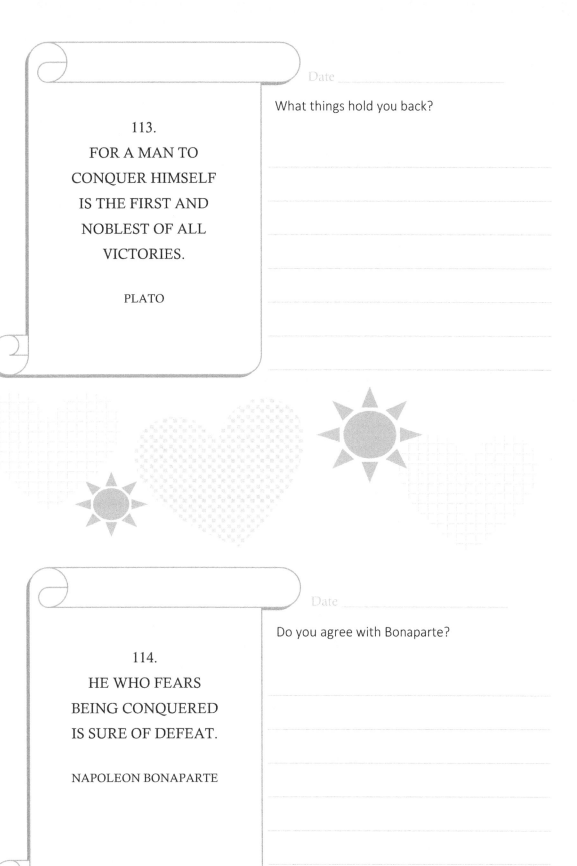

114.

HE WHO FEARS
BEING CONQUERED
IS SURE OF DEFEAT.

NAPOLEON BONAPARTE

Date _____

Do you agree with Bonaparte?

Date _____

Do you give up too easily at times?

115.
NEVER STOP TRYING.
NEVER STOP
BELIEVING.
NEVER GIVE UP.
YOUR DAY WILL COME.

UNKNOWN

Date _____

What sets your mind on fire and springs you into action?

116.
THE MIND IS NOT A
VESSEL TO BE FILLED
BUT A FIRE TO BE
KINDLED.

PLUTARCH

117.
THE FUTURE IS THE
WORST THING ABOUT
THE PRESENT.

GUSTAVE FLAUBERT

Date _____

What do you think Flaubert means by that?

118.
ONE OF THE
FIRST SIGNS OF A
SPIRIT-FILLED LIFE
IS ENTHUSIASM.

A.B. SIMPSON

Date _____

What kinds of things are you enthusiastic about?

119.
ALWAYS STAND ON
PRINCIPLE, EVEN IF
YOU STAND ALONE.

JOHN ADAMS

Has this ever happened to you, when no one
stands with you and backs you up?

120.
OUR GREATEST
ENEMIES, THE ONES
WE MUST FIGHT MOST
OFTEN, ARE WITHIN.

THOMAS PAINE

What part of your character do you fight with
most?

121.

ALWAYS VOTE FOR
PRINCIPLE, THOUGH YOU
MAY VOTE ALONE, AND
YOU MAY CHERISH THE
SWEETEST REFLECTION
THAT YOUR VOTE IS
NEVER LOST.

JOHN QUINCY ADAMS

Date _____

Do you agree with Adams?

122.

I DO THE VERY BEST
I KNOW HOW – THE VERY
BEST I CAN; AND I MEAN
TO KEEP ON DOING SO
UNTIL THE END.

ABRAHAM LINCOLN

Date _____

Do you do your very best each and every day?

123.

IF YOU WISH
TO BE LOVED,
LOVE.

SENECA

Do you allow yourself to love things freely, or
does it come with strings attached?

124.

ERRORS OF OPINION
MAY BE TOLERATED
WHERE REASON IS
LEFT FREE
TO COMBAT IT.

THOMAS JEFFERSON

What does Jefferson mean?

125.

YOU CANNOT PUSH
ANY ONE UP A LADDER
UNLESS HE BE WILLING
TO CLIMB A LITTLE
HIMSELF.

ANDREW CARNEGIE

Do you try to force people to do things because you think it's to their benefit?

126.

IGNORANT MEN RAISE
QUESTIONS THAT
WISE MEN ANSWERED
A THOUSAND
YEARS AGO.

JOHANN WOLFGANG
VON GOETHE

What does this mean to you?

127.
LIFE IS REALLY SIMPLE,
BUT WE
INSIST ON MAKING
IT COMPLICATED.

CONFUCIUS

Do you overcomplicate things?

128.
BY FAILING TO
PREPARE, YOU ARE
PREPARING TO FAIL.

BENJAMIN FRANKLIN

Do you tend to rush things and skip preparation?

Have you got hidden truths you are afraid may one day come out?

129.
TIME
DISCOVERS
TRUTH.

SENECA

Did you make a change in your routine today?

130.
THE MOST USELESS
ARE THOSE WHO
NEVER CHANGE
THROUGH THE YEARS.

JAMES M. BARRIE

Date _____

Is everything harmonious in your life?

131.
HAPPINESS IS WHEN
WHAT YOU THINK,
WHAT YOU SAY, AND
WHAT YOU DO
ARE IN HARMONY.

MAHATMA GANDHI

Date _____

Are you ready, willing, and able?

132.
KNOWING IS NOT
ENOUGH; WE MUST
APPLY. WILLING IS NOT
ENOUGH; WE MUST DO.

JOHANN WOLFGANG
VON GOETHE

Do you keep quiet to keep the peace?

133.
TO AVOID CRITICISM, DO NOTHING, SAY NOTHING, AND BE NOTHING.

ELBERT HUBBARD

Do you ever give up too easily?

134.
TRY AND FAIL, BUT DON'T FAIL TO TRY.

JOHN QUINCY ADAMS

135.

FAITH HAS TO DO WITH
THINGS THAT ARE
NOT SEEN AND
HOPE WITH THINGS
THAT ARE
NOT AT HAND.

ST. THOMAS AQUINAS

Do you suffer from wishful thinking at times?

136.

I DO NOT THINK MUCH
OF A MAN WHO IS NOT
WISER TODAY THAN
HE WAS YESTERDAY.

ABRAHAM LINCOLN

What new thing did you learn today?

Date _____

Do you let your inner child out to play?

137.

IN EVERY REAL MAN
A CHILD IS HIDDEN
THAT WANTS TO PLAY.

FRIEDRICH NIETZSCHE

Date _____

What bad habit should you quit?

138.

YOUR NET WORTH TO
THE WORLD IS USUALLY
DETERMINED BY WHAT
REMAINS AFTER YOUR
BAD HABITS ARE
SUBTRACTED FROM
YOUR GOOD ONES.

BENJAMIN FRANKLIN

Can you say the same is true in this day and age?

139.

I NEVER CONSIDERED A
DIFFERENCE OF OPINION
IN POLITICS, IN RELIGION,
IN PHILOSOPHY,
AS CAUSE FOR
WITHDRAWING
FROM A FRIEND.

THOMAS JEFFERSON

Do you aim for your highest goals?

140.

AIM FOR
THE
HIGHEST.

ANDREW CARNEGIE

141.

IF YOU WANT
TO BE HAPPY, BE.

LEO TOLSTOY

Do you allow yourself to be fully happy?

142.

WHATEVER IS WORRYING
YOU RIGHT NOW,
FORGET ABOUT IT. TAKE
A DEEP BREATH, STAY
POSITIVE AND KNOW
THAT THINGS WILL GET
BETTER.

UNKNOWN

Do you consider yourself a worrier?

Are you waiting for your ship to come in?

143.
HE THAT WAITS
UPON FORTUNE,
IS NEVER SURE
OF A DINNER.

BENJAMIN FRANKLIN

Do you make the best of circumstances, or bemoan them?

144.
THE IDEAL MAN BEARS
THE ACCIDENTS OF
LIFE WITH DIGNITY
AND GRACE, MAKING
THE BEST OF
CIRCUMSTANCES.

ARISTOTLE

145.

THE GREAT AIM OF EDUCATION IS NOT KNOWLEDGE BUT ACTION.

HERBERT SPENCER

Date _____

Do you fully act on what you've learned?

_____

_____

_____

_____

_____

_____

_____

146.

DO NOT TAKE LIFE TOO SERIOUSLY. YOU WILL NEVER GET OUT OF IT ALIVE.

ELBERT HUBBARD

Date _____

Are you guilty of being overly serious?

_____

_____

_____

_____

_____

_____

_____

147.

COURAGE AND PERSEVERANCE HAVE A MAGICAL TALISMAN, BEFORE WHICH DIFFICULTIES DISAPPEAR AND OBSTACLES VANISH INTO AIR.

JOHN QUINCY ADAMS

Date _____

Do you persevere when the going gets tough?

148.

IT IS REQUISITE FOR THE RELAXATION OF THE MIND THAT WE MAKE USE, FROM TIME TO TIME, OF PLAYFUL DEEDS AND JOKES.

ST. THOMAS AQUINAS

Date _____

Are you fun to be around?

149.

WHEN I DO GOOD
I FEEL GOOD,
WHEN I DO BAD
I FEEL BAD, AND
THAT'S MY RELIGION.

ABRAHAM LINCOLN

Date _____

Do you feel the same way as Lincoln?

150.

WHEN ONE HAS A
GREAT DEAL TO PUT
INTO IT
A DAY HAS A
HUNDRED POCKETS.

FRIEDRICH NIETZSCHE

Date _____

Do you think there are not enough hours in the day to get stuff done?

151.

LUCK IS A MATTER
OF PREPARATION
MEETING
OPPORTUNITY.

SENECA

Date _____

What were you lucky in today?

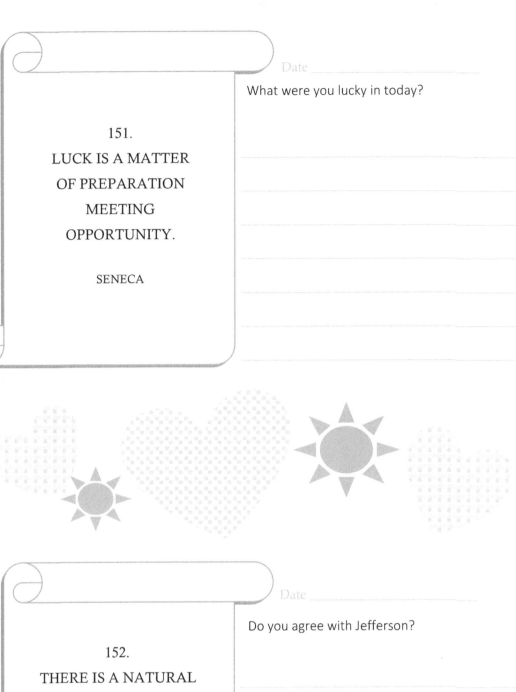

152.

THERE IS A NATURAL
ARISTOCRACY AMONG
MEN. THE GROUNDS OF
THIS ARE VIRTUE AND
TALENTS.

THOMAS JEFFERSON

Date _____

Do you agree with Jefferson?

Do you go above and beyond what's expected of you?

153.

DO YOUR DUTY
AND A LITTLE MORE
AND THE FUTURE
WILL TAKE CARE
OF ITSELF.

ANDREW CARNEGIE

What are you desirous of?

154.

LOVE AND DESIRE
ARE THE SPIRIT'S
WINGS TO
GREAT DEEDS.

JOHANN WOLFGANG
VON GOETHE

Date _____

Do you think this holds true today?

155.

THE DIRECTION IN
WHICH EDUCATION
STARTS A MAN WILL
DETERMINE HIS
FUTURE IN LIFE.

PLATO

Date _____

Do you agree with this?

156.

WHEN IT IS OBVIOUS
THAT THE GOALS
CANNOT BE REACHED,
DON'T ADJUST THE
GOALS, ADJUST THE
ACTION STEPS.

CONFUCIUS

157.

IT TAKES MANY GOOD
DEEDS TO BUILD A
GOOD REPUTATION,
AND ONLY ONE BAD
ONE TO LOSE IT.

BENJAMIN FRANKLIN

Date _____

Do you think you have to be even more careful in this day and age? Why?

158.

CHALLENGES ARE
WHAT MAKE LIFE
INTERESTING.
OVERCOMING THEM IS
WHAT MAKES THEM
MEANINGFUL.

UNKNOWN

Date _____

Do you challenge yourself enough?

159.

YOU KNOW THE VALUE OF EVERY ARTICLE OF MERCHANDISE, BUT IF YOU DON'T KNOW THE VALUE OF YOUR OWN SOUL, IT'S ALL FOOLISHNESS.

RUMI

Date _____

What do you think Rumi means?

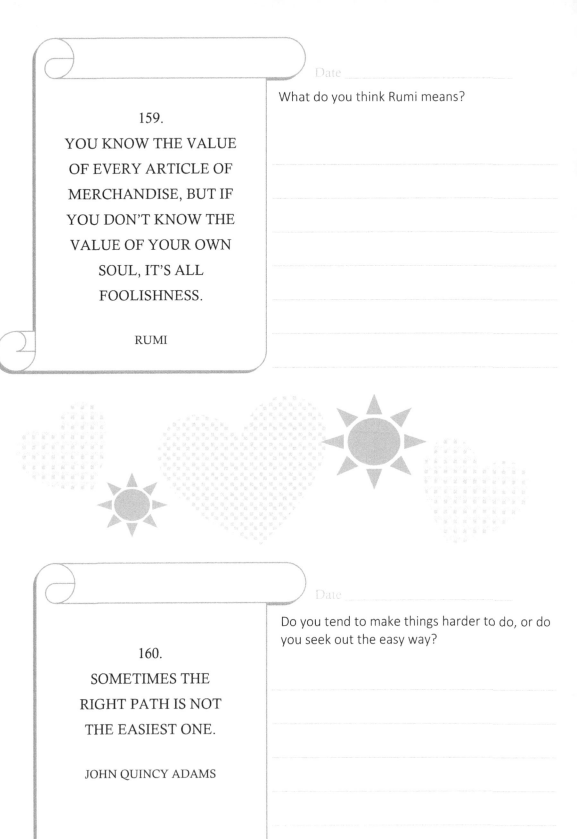

160.

SOMETIMES THE RIGHT PATH IS NOT THE EASIEST ONE.

JOHN QUINCY ADAMS

Date _____

Do you tend to make things harder to do, or do you seek out the easy way?

161.

GLANCE INTO THE WORLD JUST AS THOUGH TIME WERE GONE: AND EVERYTHING CROOKED WILL BECOME STRAIGHT TO YOU.

FRIEDRICH NIETZSCHE

Date _____

Do you tend to rush yourself in order to make decisions?

162.

IT IS NEITHER WEALTH NOR SPLENDOR; BUT TRANQUILITY AND OCCUPATION WHICH GIVE YOU HAPPINESS.

THOMAS JEFFERSON

Date _____

What makes you happy?

Do you look for the good in people / situations?

163.

THE MORE MAN
MEDITATES UPON
GOOD THOUGHTS,
THE BETTER WILL BE
HIS WORLD AND THE
WORLD AT LARGE.

CONFUCIUS

Did you make the most of today, or squander it?

164.

ONE TODAY IS WORTH
TWO TOMORROWS.

BENJAMIN FRANKLIN

Are you the master of yourself, or do others sway you?

165.

MASTERING OTHERS
IS STRENGTH.
MASTERING YOURSELF
IS TRUE POWER.

LAO TZU

Do you agree with Da Vinci?

166.

BEYOND A DOUBT
TRUTH BEARS THE
SAME RELATION TO
FALSEHOOD AS LIGHT
TO DARKNESS.

LEONARDO DA VINCI

167.

EVERY TRUTH HAS
TWO SIDES; IT IS AS
WELL TO LOOK TO
BOTH, BEFORE WE
COMMIT OURSELVES
TO EITHER.

AESOP

Date _____

Do you jump to conclusions before hearing both sides of a story?

168.

THERE IS BUT ONE
CAUSE OF HUMAN
FAILURE. AND THAT IS
MAN'S LACK OF FAITH
IN HIS TRUE SELF.

WILLIAM JAMES

Date _____

Do you have faith in yourself and your abilities?

169.
EXPERIENCE IS ONE THING YOU CAN'T GET FOR NOTHING.

OSCAR WILDE

And do you think "experience is the best teacher"?

170.
IF YOU DO NOT CHANGE DIRECTION, YOU MAY END UP WHERE YOU ARE HEADING.

LAO TZU

Do you switch track too soon and don't give enough time for something to come to fruition?

171.
ALL HAPPY FAMILIES
RESEMBLE EACH
OTHER, EACH
UNHAPPY FAMILY
IS UNHAPPY IN ITS
OWN WAY.

LEO TOLSTOY

Do you think you're responsible for your own happiness?

172.
YOU DON'T GAIN
ANYTHING FROM
STRESSING.
REMEMBER THAT.

UNKNOWN

Do you find yourself stressing out about stuff?

173.

YOU HAVE TO FIGHT
THROUGH SOME BAD
DAYS TO EARN
THE BEST DAYS OF
YOUR LIFE.

UNKNOWN

Date _____

Do you hang in there with grace when things are going wrong?

174.

THAT WHICH IS FALSE
TROUBLES THE HEART,
BUT TRUTH BRINGS
JOYOUS TRANQUILITY.

RUMI

Date _____

Do you have secrets you wish you hadn't?

175.
AS LONG AS YOU LIVE,
KEEP LEARNING
HOW TO LIVE.

SENECA

Date _____

Where do you find inspiration for your life?

_____
_____
_____
_____
_____
_____
_____

176.
HAPPINESS NEVER
DECREASES BY
BEING SHARED.

GAUTAMA BUDDHA

Date _____

Don't you love this by Buddha?

_____
_____
_____
_____
_____
_____
_____

Does making new friends come easily to you?

177.

THERE IS NOTHING ON
THIS EARTH MORE TO
BE PRIZED THAN TRUE
FRIENDSHIP.

ST. THOMAS AQUINAS

Are you the best you ... you can be?

178.

WHATEVER YOU ARE,
BE A GOOD ONE.

ABRAHAM LINCOLN

179.

THE MOMENT A PERSON FORMS A THEORY, HIS IMAGINATION SEES IN EVERY OBJECT ONLY THE TRAITS WHICH FAVOR THAT THEORY.

THOMAS JEFFERSON

Date _____

Do you agree with Jefferson?

180.

THINK OF YOURSELF AS ON THE THRESHOLD OF UNPARALLELED SUCCESS. A WHOLE, CLEAR, GLORIOUS LIFE LIES BEFORE YOU. ACHIEVE! ACHIEVE!

ANDREW CARNEGIE

Date _____

Do you have a clear vision of what your future could (and will) be?

Do you love your job?

181.

PLEASURE IN THE JOB
PUTS PERFECTION IN
THE WORK.

ARISTOTLE

Do you agree with Goethe?

182.

LOVE DOES
NOT DOMINATE;
IT CULTIVATES.

JOHANN WOLFGANG
VON GOETHE

183.

GOOD PEOPLE DO NOT NEED LAWS TO TELL THEM TO ACT RESPONSIBLY, WHILE BAD PEOPLE WILL FIND A WAY AROUND THE LAWS.

PLATO

Do you think this holds true, in this day and age?

184.

EVERYONE BELIEVES VERY EASILY WHATEVER THEY FEAR OR DESIRE.

JEAN DE LA FONTAINE

What do you fear, and desire, the most?

185.

WE BUILD TOO MANY
WALLS AND NOT
ENOUGH BRIDGES.

ISAAC NEWTON

Date _____

Do you build walls around yourself in self-protection?

186.

RICHES DO NOT
CONSIST IN THE
POSSESSION OF
TREASURES, BUT IN
THE USE
MADE OF THEM.

NAPOLEON BONAPARTE

Date _____

Do you buy stuff on the spur of the moment and regret it later –when it sits – collecting dust?

Date _____

Do you waste money?

187.

BEWARE OF LITTLE
EXPENSES. A SMALL
LEAK WILL SINK A
GREAT SHIP.

BENJAMIN FRANKLIN

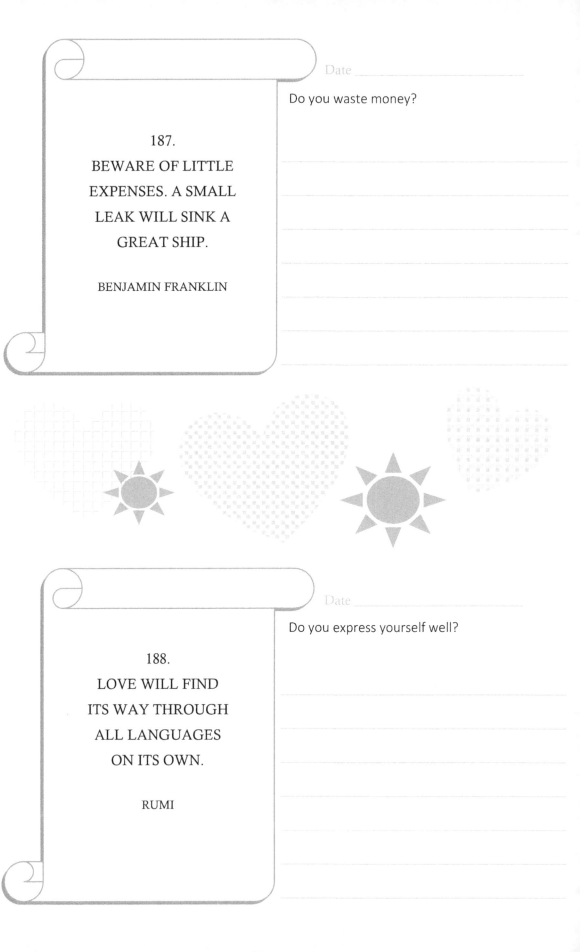

Date _____

Do you express yourself well?

188.

LOVE WILL FIND
ITS WAY THROUGH
ALL LANGUAGES
ON ITS OWN.

RUMI

189.

YOU WILL NEVER DO
ANYTHING IN THIS
WORLD WITHOUT
COURAGE. IT IS THE
GREATEST QUALITY
OF THE MIND
NEXT TO HONOR.

ARISTOTLE

Date _____

Did you show an act of courage today?

190.

EXPERIENCE DOES NOT
ERR. ONLY YOUR
JUDGMENTS ERR BY
EXPECTING FROM HER
WHAT IS NOT IN HER
POWER.

LEONARDO DA VINCI

Date _____

Do you often second-guess yourself?

191.

THE STRONG MAN IS
THE ONE WHO IS ABLE
TO INTERCEPT AT WILL
THE COMMUNICATION
BETWEEN THE SENSES
AND THE MIND.

NAPOLEON BONAPARTE

Date _____

Do you agree with Bonaparte?

192.

PLODDIING

WINS

THE

RACE.

AESOP

Date _____

Are you a slow mover, or a fast mover, once
you've made a decision?

Do you make a difference in other people's lives?

193.
ACT AS IF WHAT YOU
DO MAKES A
DIFFERENCE.
IT DOES.

WILLIAM JAMES

Do you find yourself apologizing too often?

194.
IT IS EASIER TO DO A
JOB RIGHT
THAN TO EXPLAIN
WHY YOU DIDN'T.

MARTIN VAN BUREN

Are you setting yourself up for success, or failure?

195.
SUCCESS IS A SCIENCE;
IF YOU HAVE THE
CONDITIONS,
YOU GET THE RESULT.

OSCAR WILDE

Do you live in a state of tranquility?

196.
PEACE IS
LIBERTY IN
TRANQUILITY.

CICERO

Can you back out, with grace?

197.

HE WILL WIN WHO
KNOWS WHEN TO
FIGHT AND
WHEN NOT TO FIGHT.

SUN TZU

Do you make excuses for yourself, or for others?

198.

IT IS BETTER TO OFFER
NO EXCUSE THAN A
BAD ONE.

GEORGE WASHINGTON

Date _____

Do you agree with Tolstoy?

199.
TWO OF THE MOST
POWERFUL WARRIORS
ARE
PATIENCE
AND TIME.

LEO TOLSTOY

Date _____

Do you have the inner faith that things will always turn out right?

200.
STAYING POSITIVE DOES
NOT MEAN THAT THINGS
WILL TURN OUT OKAY.
RATHER IT IS KNOWING
THAT YOU WILL BE OKAY
NO MATTER HOW THINGS
TURN OUT.

UNKNOWN

Date _____

How many minutes did you LOSE today?

201.

FOR EVERY MINUTE
YOU ARE ANGRY YOU
LOSE SIXTY SECONDS
OF HAPPINESS.

RALPH WALDO EMERSON

_____

_____

_____

_____

_____

_____

_____

Date _____

How many books a month do you read?

202.

READING IS TO THE
MIND WHAT EXERCISE
IS TO THE BODY.

JOSEPH ADDISON

_____

_____

_____

_____

_____

_____

_____

Do you often say more than is necessary?

203.

THE SUPERIOR MAN
IS MODEST IN HIS
SPEECH, BUT EXCEEDS
IN HIS ACTIONS.

CONFUCIUS

Do you agree with Franklin?

204.

WELL DONE IS BETTER
THAN WELL SAID.

BENJAMIN FRANKLIN

205.

TO KEEP THE BODY IN GOOD HEALTH IS A DUTY... OTHERWISE WE SHALL NOT BE ABLE TO KEEP OUR MIND STRONG AND CLEAR.

GAUTAMA BUDDHA

Date _____

Do you take good care of yourself?

206.

IDLENESS IS SWEET, AND ITS CONSEQUENCES ARE CRUEL.

JOHN QUINCY ADAMS

Date _____

Do you consider yourself lazy, at times?

207.

HAPPINESS IS SECURED
THROUGH VIRTUE;
IT IS A GOOD
ATTAINED BY
MAN'S OWN WILL.

ST. THOMAS AQUINAS

Date _____

Are you happy in your life choices so far?

_____

_____

_____

_____

_____

_____

208.

DON'T WORRY WHEN
YOU ARE NOT
RECOGNIZED, BUT
STRIVE TO BE WORTHY
OF RECOGNITION.

ABRAHAM LINCOLN

Date _____

Do you get the recognition you think you deserve?

_____

_____

_____

_____

_____

Date _____

Do you think this quote is true?

209.

WE OFTEN REFUSE TO
ACCEPT AN IDEA
MERELY BECAUSE THE
TONE OF VOICE IN
WHICH IT HAS BEEN
EXPRESSED IS
UNSYMPATHETIC TO US.

FRIEDRICH NIETZSCHE

Date _____

Do you think you wish for too much and are
easily disappointed when it doesn't happen?

210.

EXPECTING IS THE
GREATEST IMPEDIMENT
TO LIVING.
IN ANTICIPATION
OF TOMORROW,
IT LOSES TODAY.

SENECA

211.

NOTHING GIVES ONE PERSON SO MUCH ADVANTAGE OVER ANOTHER AS TO REMAIN ALWAYS COOL AND UNRUFFLED UNDER ALL CIRCUMSTANCES.

THOMAS JEFFERSON

Date _____

Do you lose your cool easily?

212.

IF YOU WISH TO KNOW THE MIND OF A MAN, LISTEN TO HIS WORDS.

JOHANN WOLFGANG VON GOETHE

Date _____

Are you a good listener?

Does love bring out the inner poet in you?

213.
AT THE TOUCH OF
LOVE EVERYONE
BECOMES A POET.

PLATO

What do you have to be grateful for today?

214.
GRATITUDE IS NOT
ONLY THE GREATEST
OF VIRTUES,
BUT THE PARENT OF
ALL THE OTHERS.

CICERO

215.

**LOOK BACK,
AND SMILE
ON PERILS PAST.**

WALTER SCOTT

Can you let the past go?

216.

**SUCCESS DEPENDS
UPON PREVIOUS
PREPARATION, AND
WITHOUT SUCH
PREPARATION THERE
IS SURE TO BE FAILURE.**

CONFUCIUS

How well do you prepare for something important?

Did you say something tactless today?

217.
TACT IS THE ART OF
MAKING A POINT
WITHOUT MAKING
AN ENEMY.

ISAAC NEWTON

Do you waste time, or make good use of time?

218.
TIME BIDES LONG
ENOUGH FOR THOSE
WHO MAKE USE OF IT.

LEONARDO DA VINCI

Do you make mountains out of molehills?

219.

IMPOSSIBLE IS A WORD
TO BE FOUND ONLY
IN THE DICTIONARY
OF FOOLS.

NAPOLEON BONAPARTE

Did you do a random act of kindness. Today?

220.

NO ACT
OF KINDNESS,
NO MATTER
HOW SMALL,
IS EVER WASTED.

AESOP

221.
I'VE GOT BIG SHOES
TO FILL. THIS IS MY
CHANCE TO DO
SOMETHING.
I HAVE TO
SEIZE THE MOMENT.

ANDREW JACKSON

What did you step up and do that was not expected of you?

222.
EXPERIENCE IS SIMPLY
THE NAME WE GIVE
OUR MISTAKES.

OSCAR WILDE

Did you learn from any mistakes today?

Do you plan or fly by the seat of your pants?

223.
BEFORE BEGINNING,
PLAN CAREFULLY.

CICERO

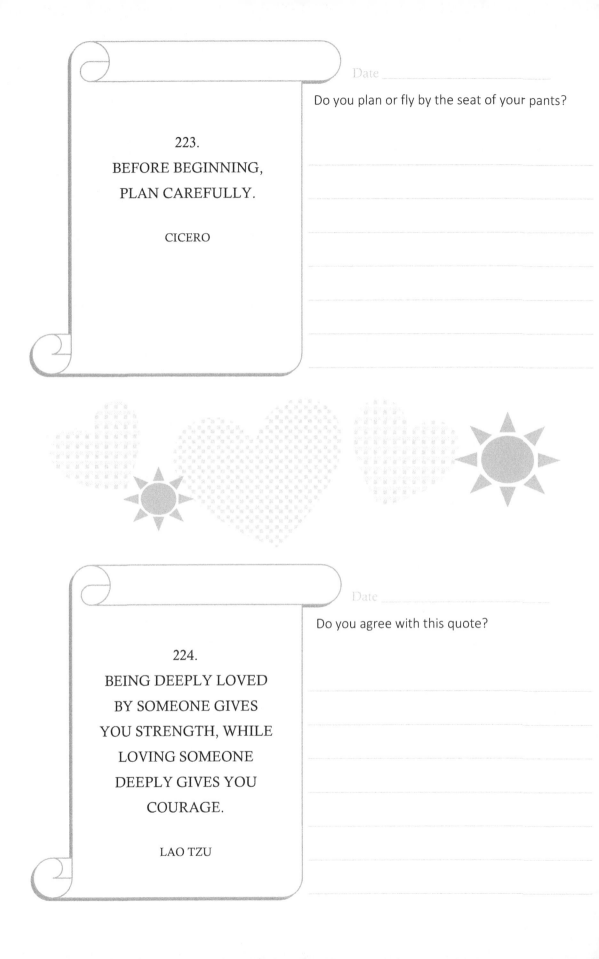

Do you agree with this quote?

224.
BEING DEEPLY LOVED
BY SOMEONE GIVES
YOU STRENGTH, WHILE
LOVING SOMEONE
DEEPLY GIVES YOU
COURAGE.

LAO TZU

225.
IT IS BETTER TO BE ALONE THAN IN BAD COMPANY.

GEORGE WASHINGTON

Do you prefer to be alone when you're in a bad mood?

226.
EVERYONE THINKS OF CHANGING THE WORLD, BUT NO ONE THINKS OF CHANGING HIMSELF.

LEO TOLSTOY

Michael Jackson's "Man in the Mirror" comes to mind here. What does this quote mean to you?

Is your soul a "noble soul" because you're grateful?

227.

GRATITUDE IS THE
SIGN OF NOBLE SOULS.

AESOP

If "you are what you eat" is true, "what we think" must also be true?

228.

WE ARE SHAPED BY
OUR THOUGHTS,
WE BECOME
WHAT WE THINK.

GAUTAMA BUDDHA

229.

THE REAL MAN SMILES
IN TROUBLE,
GATHERS STRENGTH
FROM DISTRESS,
AND GROWS BRAVE
BY REFLECTION.

THOMAS PAINE

Date _____

Do you give in and smile when things are going awry?

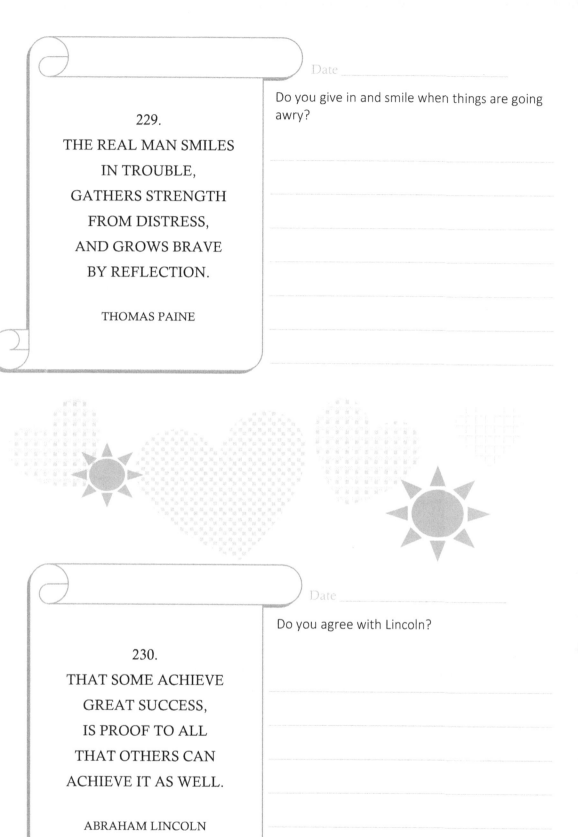

230.

THAT SOME ACHIEVE
GREAT SUCCESS,
IS PROOF TO ALL
THAT OTHERS CAN
ACHIEVE IT AS WELL.

ABRAHAM LINCOLN

Date _____

Do you agree with Lincoln?

What was a good deed you did today?
And for whom?

231.

HE THAT DOES GOOD
TO ANOTHER DOES
GOOD ALSO TO
HIMSELF.

SENECA

What are your dreams for your future?

232.

I LIKE THE DREAMS OF
THE FUTURE BETTER
THAN THE HISTORY
OF THE PAST.

THOMAS JEFFERSON

233.

ONLY BY JOY AND
SORROW DOES A PERSON
KNOW ANYTHING ABOUT
THEMSELVES AND THEIR
DESTINY. THEY LEARN
WHAT TO DO AND WHAT
TO AVOID.

JOHANN WOLFGANG

Date _____

What, from your past, have you learned to avoid repeating in the future?

234.

WHEN THE MIND IS
THINKING IT IS
TALKING TO ITSELF.

PLATO

Date _____

Do you ever accidentally think "out loud"?

Are you a whiner, a complainer?
Or the opposite?

235.
ANY FOOL CAN
CRITICIZE, CONDEMN
AND COMPLAIN – AND
MOST FOOLS DO.

BENJAMIN FRANKLIN

Do you grieve for things lost?

236.
DON'T GRIEVE.
ANYTHING YOU LOSE
COMES ROUND IN
ANOTHER FORM.

RUMI

What new thing did you learn today?

237.

LEARNING NEVER
EXHAUSTS THE MIND.

LEONARDO DA VINCI

Do you tend to "love more" or "hate more"?

238.

A TRUE MAN
HATES NO ONE.

NAPOLEON BONAPARTE

239.
YOUR MIND IS A
POWERFUL THING.
WHEN YOU FILL IT
WITH POSITIVE
THOUGHTS,
YOUR LIFE WILL
START TO CHANGE.

UNKNOWN

Are you a positive thinker?

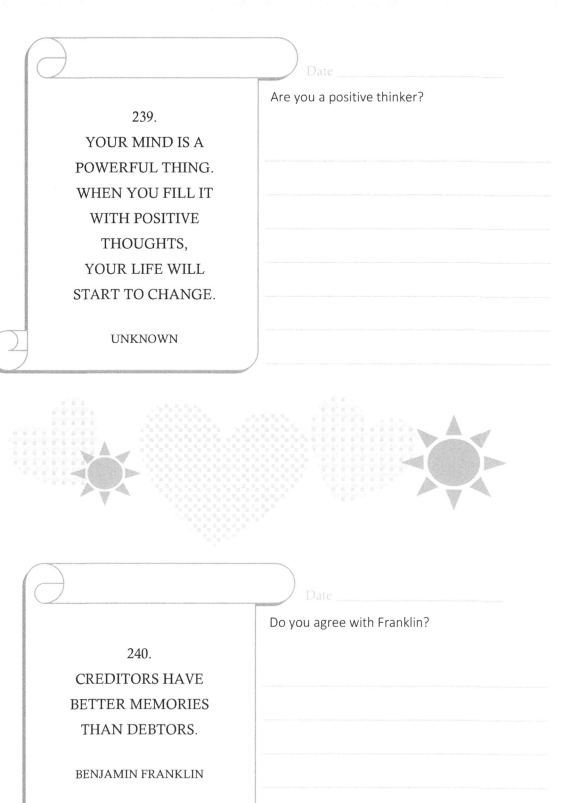

240.
CREDITORS HAVE
BETTER MEMORIES
THAN DEBTORS.

BENJAMIN FRANKLIN

Do you agree with Franklin?

241.

IF CONSCIENCE
DISAPPROVES, THE
LOUDEST APPLAUSES
OF THE WORLD ARE OF
LITTLE VALUE.

JOHN ADAMS

Do you think you should only be rewarded by a job well done?

242.

SUCCESS OR FAILURE
IN BUSINESS IS
CAUSED MORE BY THE
MENTAL ATTITUDE
EVEN THAN BY
MENTAL CAPACITIES.

WALTER SCOTT

If you're in business, do you have the right mental attitude to succeed?

Date _____

Do you love yourself enough?

243.

TO LOVE ONESELF IS
THE BEGINNING OF A
LIFELONG ROMANCE.

OSCAR WILDE

Date _____

Do you agree with Seneca?

244.

NO GREAT GENIUS
HAS EVER EXISTED
WITHOUT SOME
TOUCH OF MADNESS.

SENECA

Are you planning an adventure any time soon?

245.
ADVENTURE IS
WORTHWHILE.

AESOP

Do you agree with this quote?

246.
A GREAT MANY
PEOPLE THINK THEY
ARE THINKING WHEN
THEY ARE MERELY
REARRANGING THEIR
PREJUDICES.

WILLIAM JAMES

Do you know "what not to fear"?

247.
COURAGE IS KNOWING
WHAT NOT TO FEAR.

PLATO

What's your analogy for Rumi's quote?

248.
IF YOU FIND THE
MIRROR OF THE HEART
DULL, THE RUST HAS
NOT BEEN CLEARED
FROM ITS FACE.

RUMI

How many close friends do you have?

249.

LOVE IS THE
ATTEMPT TO FORM
A FRIENDSHIP
INSPIRED BY BEAUTY.

CICERO

Are you wise, or a fool?

250.

WISE MEN
DON'T NEED ADVICE.
FOOLS WON'T TAKE IT.

BENJAMIN FRANKLIN

251.

NO MAN IS RICH
ENOUGH TO
BUY BACK HIS PAST.

OSCAR WILDE

Date _____

What would you want to buy back (and change) from your past if you could?

252.

EVERY ACTION NEEDS
TO BE PROMPTED
BY A MOTIVE.

LEONARDO DA VINCI

Date _____

What gets you out of bed in the morning?

Date _____

Are you overly-protective of loved ones?

253.

IF THE HIGHEST AIM OF
A CAPTAIN WERE TO
PRESERVE HIS SHIP, HE
WOULD LEAVE IT
IN PORT FOREVER.

ST. THOMAS AQUINAS

Date _____

Have you ever been so angry as to feel ill after a disagreement?

254.

CONSIDER, WHEN YOU
ARE ENRAGED AT
ANY ONE, WHAT YOU
WOULD PROBABLY
THINK IF HE SHOULD
DIE DURING THE
DISPUTE.

SENECA

Date _____

Do you think you know everything? ;-)

255.
TO KNOW
WHAT YOU KNOW
AND WHAT
YOU DO NOT KNOW,
THAT IS TRUE
KNOWLEDGE.

CONFUCIUS

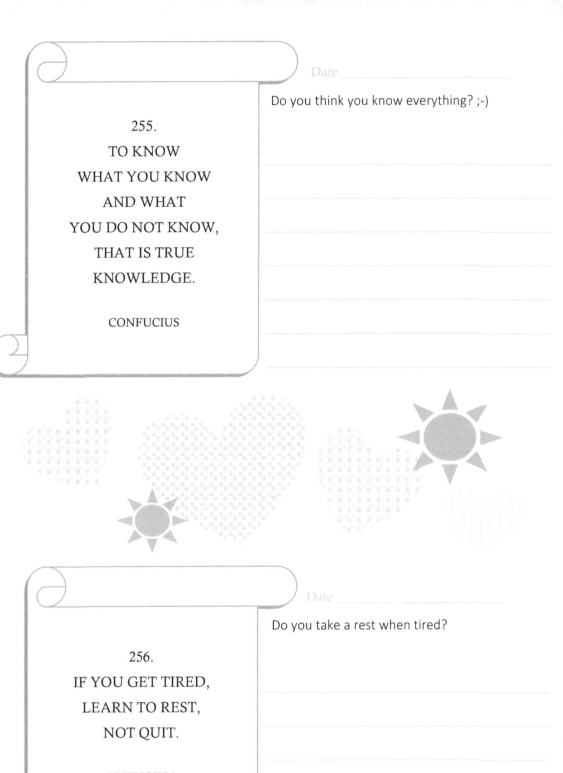

Date _____

Do you take a rest when tired?

256.
IF YOU GET TIRED,
LEARN TO REST,
NOT QUIT.

UNKNOWN

257.

THIS LIFE IS WORTH
LIVING, WE CAN SAY,
SINCE IT IS
WHAT WE MAKE IT.

WILLIAM JAMES

Do you make the best of any given circumstance?

258.

COMMON SENSE IS
THAT WHICH JUDGES
THE THINGS GIVEN TO
IT BY OTHER SENSES.

LEONARDO DA VINCI

Date

Do you agree with da Vinci?

259.
GOVERNING A GREAT
NATION IS LIKE
COOKING A SMALL
FISH – TOO MUCH
HANDLING
WILL SPOIL IT.

LAO TZU

Date _____

Do you ever feel over-regulated, by your job,
or family members?

260.
MOST PEOPLE ARE AS
HAPPY AS THEY MAKE
UP THEIR MINDS TO BE.

ABRAHAM LINCOLN

Date _____

Are YOU happy?
Do you allow yourself to BE happy?

261.
THE HERD SEEK OUT
THE GREAT, NOT FOR
THEIR SAKE BUT FOR
THEIR INFLUENCE;
AND THE GREAT
WELCOME THEM OUT
OF VANITY OR NEED.

NAPOLEON BONAPARTE

Date _____

Are you easily influenced by others?

262.
DIFFICULTIES
STRENGTHEN
THE MIND,
AS LABOR DOES
THE BODY.

SENECA

Date _____

Do you agree with Seneca?

263.

IN AMERICA THE YOUNG
ARE ALWAYS READY TO
GIVE TO THOSE WHO ARE
OLDER THAN
THEMSELVES THE FULL
BENEFITS OF THEIR
INEXPERIENCE.

OSCAR WILDE

Date _____

Do you take notice of "youngsters" opinions?

264.

IT'S EASIER TO RESIST
AT THE BEGINNING
THAN AT THE END.

LEONARDO DA VINCI

Date _____

What did you do recently that you wish you
hadn't started?

265.

GREAT EMERGENCIES
AND CRISES SHOW US
HOW MUCH GREATER
OUR VITAL RESOURCES
ARE THAN WE HAD
SUPPOSED.

WILLIAM JAMES

Date _____

What crisis have you overcome recently and come out stronger?

266.

DILIGENCE IS THE
MOTHER OF
GOOD LUCK.

BENJAMIN FRANKLIN

Date _____

Do you feel like a "lucky" person?

267.

I BELIEVE THAT EVERY
HUMAN MIND FEELS
PLEASURE IN DOING
GOOD TO ANOTHER.

THOMAS JEFFERSON

Date _____

Did you do something nice and unexpected for someone today?

268.

THE HUMAN RACE IS
GOVERNED BY ITS
IMAGINATION.

NAPOLEON BONAPARTE

Date _____

What imaginative thing did you do at work today?

269.

HE WHO ENJOYS
DOING AND ENJOYS
WHAT HE HAS DONE
IS HAPPY.

JOHANN WOLFGANG
VON GOETHE

Date _____

What did you get done today that made you happy?

270.

THERE IS NO HARM
IN REPEATING
A GOOD THING.

PLATO

Date _____

Do you agree with Plato?

Are you satisfied with what you have or are you always "wanting more"?

271.
I HAVE THE SIMPLEST
TASTES. I AM ALWAYS
SATISFIED WITH
THE BEST.

OSCAR WILDE

Did you try, yet fail, in something today?

272.
IF THOU ART A MAN,
ADMIRE THOSE WHO
ATTEMPT GREAT
THINGS, EVEN THOUGH
THEY FAIL.

SENECA

Did you take advantage of an opportunity that came your way today?

273.

ABILITY IS NOTHING
WITHOUT
OPPORTUNITY.

NAPOLEON BONAPARTE

Do you agree with Confucius?

274.

VIRTUE IS NOT LEFT
TO STAND ALONE.
HE WHO PRACTICES IT
WILL HAVE
NEIGHBORS.

CONFUCIUS

275.

HE THAT IS OF THE OPINION MONEY WILL DO EVERYTHING MAY WELL BE SUSPECTED OF DOING EVERYTHING FOR MONEY.

BENJAMIN FRANKLIN

Date _____

Do you think this is true?

276.

WE DON'T LAUGH BECAUSE WE'RE HAPPY - WE'RE HAPPY BECAUSE WE LAUGH.

WILLIAM JAMES

Date _____

Did you have a good laugh today?

277.

ALL OUR KNOWLEDGE HAS ITS ORIGINS IN OUR PERCEPTIONS.

LEONARDO DA VINCI

Date _____

Do you believe everything you read?

278.

THE PURSUIT, EVEN OF THE BEST THINGS, OUGHT TO BE CALM AND TRANQUIL.

CICERO

Date _____

Do you go about your pursuits in a calm and meaningful way, or like a bull in a china shop?

279.

**TO SEE THINGS IN THE
SEED, THAT IS GENIUS.**

LAO TZU

Date _____

Did you have big idea spring from a small thought today?

280.

**BEAUTY
SURROUNDS US,
BUT USUALLY WE
NEED TO BE WALKING
IN A GARDEN TO
KNOW IT.**

RUMI

Date _____

Did you take time to smell the roses today?

281.

TO THE TIMID AND
HESITATING
EVERYTHING IS
IMPOSSIBLE BECAUSE
IT SEEMS SO.

WALTER SCOTT

Date _____

Do you sometimes feel that things are
impossible for you to achieve in life?

282.

WRITE INJURIES
IN DUST,
BENEFITS IN MARBLE.

BENJAMIN FRANKLIN

Date _____

Does this quote ring true for you?

Can you start a project and leave it undone without a guilty conscience?

283.
FACED WITH
WHAT IS RIGHT,
TO LEAVE IT UNDONE
SHOWS A LACK OF
COURAGE.

CONFUCIUS

If you have the right answer, do you always share it?

284.
HE WHO KNOWS,
DOES NOT SPEAK.
HE WHO SPEAKS,
DOES NOT KNOW.

LAO TZU

285.

IF YOU WANT
A QUALITY,
ACT AS IF YOU
ALREADY HAD IT.

WILLIAM JAMES

What quality do you lack and wish to acquire?

286.

LOST TIME IS NEVER
FOUND AGAIN.

BENJAMIN FRANKLIN

How much time did you waste today?

287.
MAN'S ENEMIES
ARE NOT DEMONS,
BUT HUMAN BEINGS
LIKE HIMSELF.

LAO TZU

Date _____

Do you have any hidden demons?

288.
IF I HAVE DONE THE
PUBLIC ANY SERVICE,
IT IS DUE TO MY
PATIENT THOUGHT.

ISAAC NEWTON

Date _____

Can you patiently think things through, or do you rush making decisions?

Date _____

Do people think you're opinionated?

289.
THE GREATEST
DECEPTION MEN
SUFFER IS FROM
THEIR OWN OPINIONS.

LEONARD DA VINCI

Date _____

Do you agree with Bonaparte?

290.
COURAGE
IS LIKE LOVE;
IT MUST HAVE HOPE
FOR NOURISHMENT.

NAPOLEON BONAPARTE

291.

BE SLOW IN
CHOOSING A FRIEND,
SLOWER IN CHANGING.

BENJAMIN FRANKLIN

Do you have more friends today, than you did in high school?

292.

THE LITTLE REED,
BENDING TO THE
FORCE OF THE WIND,
SOON STOOD UPRIGHT
AGAIN WHEN THE
STORM HAD PASSED
OVER.

AESOP

Do you weather (personal) storms well?

Date _____

Are you content today?

293.
HE WHO IS
CONTENTED
IS RICH.

LAO TZU

Date _____

Do you believe that life is worth living?

294.
BELIEVE THAT LIFE
IS WORTH LIVING
AND YOUR BELIEF
WILL HELP CREATE
THE FACT.

WILLIAM JAMES

Date _____

Do you agree with Jackson?

295.
YOU MUST PAY THE
PRICE IF YOU WISH TO
SECURE THE BLESSING.

ANDREW JACKSON

Date _____

Which class do you consider yourself to be in?

296.
THE WORLD IS DIVIDED
INTO TWO CLASSES,
THOSE WHO BELIEVE
THE INCREDIBLE,
AND THOSE WHO DO
THE IMPROBABLE.

OSCAR WILDE

Have you ever "looked the other way"?

297.

TO SEE THE RIGHT
AND NOT TO DO IT
IS COWARDICE.

CONFUCIUS

How easily do you learn from your mistakes?

298.

ANY MAN
CAN MAKE MISTAKES,
BUT ONLY AN IDIOT
PERSISTS IN HIS ERROR.

CICERO

Do you find yourself creating "busy work"?

299.

NEVER CONFUSE
MOTION WITH ACTION.

BENJAMIN FRANKLIN

Do you feel you receive proper credit /
acknowledgement for work done?

300.

WHEN THE BEST
LEADER'S WORK
IS DONE
THE PEOPLE SAY,
'WE DID IT
OURSELVES.'

LAO TZU

Do you crave fame?

301.
HUSTLE UNTIL
YOU NO LONGER HAVE
TO INTRODUCE
YOURSELF.

UNKNOWN

Do you take chances without any prep work?

302.
I WILL PREPARE AND
SOME DAY MY CHANCE
WILL COME.

ABRAHAM LINCOLN

Do you make truly loving someone / something a daily habit?

303.

WE LOVE LIFE,
NOT BECAUSE WE ARE
USED TO LIVING BUT
BECAUSE WE ARE USED
TO LOVING.

FRIEDRICH NIETZSCHE

Do you agree with Franklin?

304.

LIFE'S TRAGEDY
IS THAT WE
GET TOO OLD TOO SOON
AND WISE TOO LATE.

BENJAMIN FRANKLIN

Do you seek out advice from wise souls?

305.

NO MAN WAS EVER
WISE BY CHANCE.

SENECA

Do you have the right education to go after your dreams?

306.

THE EXPECTATIONS OF
LIFE DEPEND UPON
DILIGENCE; THE
MECHANIC THAT
WOULD PERFECT HIS
WORK MUST FIRST
SHARPEN HIS TOOLS.

CONFUCIUS

Date _____

Do you know what to overlook on a daily basis?

307.
THE ART OF BEING
WISE IS THE ART OF
KNOWING WHAT TO
OVERLOOK.

WILLIAM JAMES

Date _____

How much time did you waste today?

308.
A LIFE OF LEISURE AND
A LIFE OF LAZINESS
ARE TWO THINGS.
THERE WILL BE
SLEEPING ENOUGH IN
THE GRAVE.

BENJAMIN FRANKLIN

309.
WHERE THERE
IS SHOUTING,
THERE IS NO TRUE
KNOWLEDGE.

LEONARDO DA VINCI

Date _____

What do you think da Vinci means?

310.
THE POWER OF
INTUITIVE
UNDERSTANDING WILL
PROTECT YOU FROM
HARM UNTIL THE END
OF YOUR DAYS.

LAO TZU

Date _____

Can you think on your feet when you have to make a quick decision?

Date _____

Do you seek out the best in people?

311.

NEVER CONTRACT
FRIENDSHIP WITH
A MAN THAT IS NOT
BETTER THAN
THYSELF.

CONFUCIUS

Date _____

Do you find it easy to get people to see things
your way?

312.

PERSUASION IS OFTEN
MORE EFFECTUAL
THAN FORCE.

AESOP

313.
VICTORY BELONGS
TO THE MOST
PERSEVERING.

NAPOLEON BONAPARTE

Date _____

Can you hang in there during hard / difficult times?

314.
WHEN YOU'RE
FINISHED CHANGING,
YOU'RE FINISHED.

BENJAMIN FRANKLIN

Date _____

What changes in your life do you want to make?

315.
THE GREATEST WEAPON AGAINST STRESS IS OUR ABILITY TO CHOOSE ONE THOUGHT OVER ANOTHER.

WILLIAM JAMES

Date _____

Everything's a choice. Do you recognize when you've made a bad choice?

316.
ALWAYS FORGIVE YOUR ENEMIES – NOTHING ANNOYS THEM SO MUCH.

OSCAR WILDE

Date _____

Did you need to forgive someone today?

317.
NATURE DOES
NOT HURRY, YET
EVERYTHING IS
ACCOMPLISHED.

LAO TZU

Do you find yourself rushing to complete things?

318.
DON'T WAIT FOR
OPPORTUNITY.
CREATE IT.

UNKNOWN

What opportunity did you create for yourself today?

319.
EVERYBODY LIKES
A
COMPLIMENT

ABRAHAM LINCOLN

Did you hand out any compliments today?

320.
FATIGUE
IS THE BEST PILLOW.

BENJAMIN FRANKLIN

Are you fulfilled at the end of your day?

321.

IT IS MORE FITTING
FOR A MAN TO LAUGH
AT LIFE THAN TO
LAMENT OVER IT.

SENECA

Date _____

Can you laugh at yourself?

322.

WHENEVER YOU DO
A THING,
ACT AS IF ALL
THE WORLD WERE
WATCHING.

THOMAS JEFFERSON

Date _____

Do you agree with Jefferson?

Do you feel fully appreciated for all you do?

323.

THE DEEPEST
PRINCIPLE IN HUMAN
NATURE IS THE
CRAVING TO BE
APPRECIATED.

WILLIAM JAMES

Does your mirror reflect the good in you?

324.

A MAN'S MANNERS
ARE A MIRROR
IN WHICH HE SHOWS
HIS PORTRAIT.

JOHANN WOLFGANG
VON GOETHE

325.

**HE WHO KNOWS THAT
ENOUGH IS ENOUGH
WILL ALWAYS
HAVE ENOUGH.**

LAO TZU

Date _____

Do you often find yourself wishing you had more?

326.

**A MAN
WRAPPED UP
IN HIMSELF MAKES A
VERY SMALL BUNDLE.**

BENJAMIN FRANKLIN

Date _____

How wrapped up in yourself are you?

327.

I NEVER DID ANYTHING
WORTH DOING
BY ACCIDENT, NOR DID
ANY OF MY INVENTIONS
COME BY ACCIDENT;
THEY CAME BY WORK.

PLATO

Date _____

Are you always satisfied when you've finished a job / chore?

328.

WHEN ANGER RISES,
THINK OF THE
CONSEQUENCES.

CONFUCIUS

Date _____

Do you think before you speak?

329.
MY POWERS ARE
ORDINARY.
ONLY MY
APPLICATION
BRINGS ME SUCCESS.

ISAAC NEWTON

Do you always apply yourself to a given situation?

330.
NATURE NEVER
BREAKS HER OWN
LAWS.

LEONARDO DA VINCI

Do you often break your own rules?

331.

DO NOT
FEAR MISTAKES.
YOU WILL KNOW
FAILURE.
CONTINUE TO
REACH OUT.

BENJAMIN FRANKLIN

Date _____

Do you think failure makes you stronger?

332.

ONE WHO IS TOO
INSISTENT ON
HIS OWN VIEWS,
FINDS FEW TO
AGREE WITH HIM.

LAO TZU

Date _____

Do you find yourself wanting to be right all the time?

333.
A LEADER
IS A DEALER
IN HOPE.

NAPOLEON BONAPARTE

Do you exude hope around your friends and family?

334.
THE GREATEST
DISCOVERY OF MY
GENERATION IS THAT
A HUMAN BEING CAN
ALTER HIS LIFE BY
ALTERING HIS
ATTITUDES.

WILLIAM JAMES

Do you have a good, or bad, attitude in general?

Do you tend to please others first, rather than yourself first?

335.

PLEASE ALL,
AND YOU
WILL PLEASE NONE.

AESOP

Can you take decisive action when necessary?

336.

TAKE TIME TO
DELIBERATE;
BUT WHEN THE TIME
FOR ACTION ARRIVES,
STOP THINKING
AND GO IN.

ANDREW JACKSON

What does this quote make you think make you think of? At the moment we're laying this out.

337.

BLESSED IS HE THAT
EXPECTS NOTHING,
FOR HE SHALL NEVER
BE DISAPPOINTED.

BENJAMIN FRANKLIN

When you were much younger, did you think you had all the answers?

338.

THE OLD BELIEVE
EVERYTHING,
THE MIDDLE-AGED
SUSPECT EVERYTHING,
THE YOUNG KNOW
EVERYTHING.

OSCAR WILDE

339.
**LOVE IS OF ALL PASSIONS
THE STRONGEST,
FOR IT ATTACKS
SIMULTANEOUSLY
THE HEAD, THE HEART
AND THE SENSES.**

LAO TZU

Date _____

Do you think love is the strongest passion?

340.
**THE GREATER THE
DIFFICULTY,
THE GREATER
THE GLORY.**

CICERO

Date _____

Do things come easily to you, or do you find life to be "hard work" at times?

Do you find yourself "getting in your own way" when trying to succeed?

341.
YOU ARE THE
ONLY ONE
WHO CAN LIMIT
YOUR GREATNESS.

UNKNOWN

Can you accept a bad incident from the past and move on?

342.
ACCEPTANCE OF WHAT
HAS HAPPENED
IS THE FIRST STEP
TO OVERCOMING
THE CONSEQUENCES
OF ANY MISFORTUNE.

WILLIAM JAMES

Date _____

Are you at peace with yourself and your innermost thoughts?

343.

THE FIRST AND
GREATEST VICTORY
IS TO
CONQUER SELF.

PLATO

Date _____

When you get angry, is it always with reason?

344.

ANGER IS NEVER
WITHOUT A REASON,
BUT SELDOM WITH
A GOOD ONE.

BENJAMIN FRANKLIN

345.

A HAPPY LIFE
IS ONE WHICH
IS IN ACCORDANCE
WITH ITS
OWN NATURE.

SENECA

Date _____

What makes you happy in your life?

346.

LET THE BEAUTY
OF WHAT YOU LOVE
BE WHAT YOU DO.

RUMI

Date _____

What do you absolutely love to do?
And do you do it often?

347.
BECAUSE OF A
GREAT LOVE,
ONE IS COURAGEOUS.

LAO TZU

Do you consider yourself a courageous person?

348.
ALL MEN WHO HAVE
TURNED OUT
WORTH ANYTHING
HAVE HAD THE
CHIEF HAND IN THEIR
OWN EDUCATION.

WALTER SCOTT

Are you steering your own destiny by getting the right education necessary to succeed?

349.

ALL MANKIND IS DIVIDED
INTO THREE CLASSES:
THOSE THAT ARE
IMMOVABLE,
THOSE THAT ARE MOVABLE,
AND THOSE THAT MOVE.

BENJAMIN FRANKLIN

Date _____

Are you able to take action easily, or do you procrastinate?

350.

TO BE IGNORANT OF
WHAT OCCURRED
BEFORE YOU WERE
BORN IS TO REMAIN
ALWAYS A CHILD.

CICERO

Date _____

Do you know who your ancestors are, beyond your grandparents?

Date _____

351.

ACTION MAY NOT
BRING HAPPINESS
BUT THERE IS NO
HAPPINESS
WITHOUT ACTION.

WILLIAM JAMES

When you take action , does it bring you
happiness?

Date _____

352.

TO EXPECT THE
UNEXPECTED
SHOWS A
THOROUGHLY
MODERN INTELLECT.

OSCAR WILDE

Do you like, or hate, the fact that you don't
know what's around the next corner?

353.
YOU CANNOT
OPEN A BOOK
WITHOUT LEARNING
SOMETHING.

CONFUCIUS

Date _____

What educational book are you currently reading?

354.
IF YOU WOULD KNOW
THE VALUE OF MONEY,
GO AND TRY TO
BORROW SOME.

BENJAMIN FRANKLIN

Date _____

Are you good with money?

Do you let perfectionism to get in the way of getting the job done?

355.
DON'T TRY TO
BE PERFECT.
JUST TRY TO BE BETTER
THAN YOU WERE
YESTERDAY.

UNKNOWN

Do you regret spending time learning stuff that you no longer have the need for?

356.
THE NATURAL DESIRE
OF GOOD MEN
IS KNOWLEDGE.

LEONARDO DA VINCI

Date _____

Do you agree with Aesop?

357.
IT IS EASY
TO BE BRAVE
FROM A
SAFE DISTANCE.

AESOP

Date _____

What good deeds did you do today?

358.
GREAT ACTS
ARE MADE UP OF
SMALL DEEDS.

LAO TZU

359.

YOU CAN HAVE NO
DOMINION GREATER
OR LESS THAN THAT
OVER YOURSELF.

LEONARDO DA VINCI

Date _____

Do you feel like you're in control of yourself, or do you allow others to control you?

360.

A GOOD CONSCIENCE
IS A CONTINUAL
CHRISTMAS.

BENJAMIN FRANKLIN

Date _____

Do you have a good conscience, on this Christmas Day?

361.
LIFE'S LIKE A PLAY; IT'S NOT THE LENGTH, BUT THE EXCELLENCE OF THE ACTING THAT MATTERS.

SENECA

Date _____

Are you living your life to the fullest? If not, what changes are you going to make next year?

362.
A CHAIN IS NO STRONGER THAN ITS WEAKEST LINK, AND LIFE IS AFTER ALL A CHAIN.

WILLIAM JAMES

Date _____

Do you think life is just a chain of events?

Date _____

363.

THERE ARE MANY
THINGS WE WOULD
THROW AWAY IF WE
WERE NOT AFRAID
THAT OTHERS MIGHT
PICK THEM UP.

OSCAR WILDE

Does this ring true for you?

Date _____

364.

IF YOU WANT IT,
YOU'LL FIND A WAY.
IF YOU DON'T,
YOU'LL FIND AN
EXCUSE.

UNKNOWN

What was the last thing you were determined to get and succeeded in acquiring?

Date _____

Do you talk about people behind their backs?

365.

SPEAK ILL OF NO MAN,
BUT SPEAK ALL THE
GOOD YOU KNOW OF
EVERYBODY.

BENJAMIN FRANKLIN

Date _____

What are you going to do with this extra day?

AN EXTRA DAY to account
FOR LEAP YEAR

DAY 366.

TO BE WRONGED
IS NOTHING UNLESS
YOU CONTINUE
TO REMEMBER IT.

CONFUCIUS

Made in the USA
Monee, IL
29 November 2022